LYDIA

Christian Businesswoman

Katherine Greegor

Illustrated by
Bill Perry

BARBOUR
PUBLISHING

© 1995 by Barbour Publishing, Inc.

ISBN 1-58660-948-3

Published by Barbour Publishing, Inc., P.O. Box 719, Uhrichsville, Ohio 44683, www.barbourbooks.com

ecpa Member of the
Evangelical Christian
Publishers Association

Printed in the United States of America.
5 4 3 2 1

LYDIA

"SHE'S JUST OUTSIDE THE DOOR AGAIN."

1

MARKETPLACE

"Mother, what should I do?" whispered young Alexander. "She's just outside the door again."

Lydia sighed as she glanced up from the vat into which old Lucius had moments before dipped the woolen yarn. Nodding towards a young worker who had just finished crushing the shells of the murex shellfish that would later be boiled to make more purple dye, Lydia directed, "Keep all the workers busy." Rushing through the curtained doorway, Lydia dashed through the shop and into the marketplace.

Old Lucius grinned a big, toothless grin and gave Alexander a knowing wink. "Someone's in big trouble now. I surely wouldn't want that woman on my case."

Lydia no sooner was out in the open air than she heard, "Tell your fortune? Just two pennies to learn of your future."

"Phebe, listen to me. You know I will not have my fortune told, so please do not ask again," Lydia pleaded with exasperation. "Now where is Dimitri?"

Phebe shrugged her shoulders. Lydia was sure Phebe knew where her master was but couldn't tell because she feared a severe beating from either Dimitri or Spiro. Neither would think twice about beating the ragged slave girl if she dared to disobey in any way. So Lydia picked up the folds of her tunic and made her way into the colorful early morning crowds that were gathering to begin the day's business.

Tables with a vast array of merchandise, meat,

"WATCH WHERE YOU'RE GOING, LADY!"

and produce were quickly filling all the available space in the marketplace. In her haste, Lydia nearly knocked some pottery off a counter when her tunic caught the corner of the table. "Watch where you're going, lady! Do you have enough money to pay for all of this?" the angry merchant cried as he waved his hands through the air.

She offered a quick apology and continued her search for Dimitri or Spiro. Being short and plump, Dimitri could easily disappear in a crowd. Spiro was taller—as a matter of fact, slightly taller than almost anyone in the crowd—and Lydia hoped she would be able to spot his graying hair above that of the other merchants and shoppers. Sure enough, as she rounded the corner to the street of the bakers, she spotted the crop of curly gray hair that she recognized as Spiro's and set off with determination towards him.

"Spiro, you must keep Phebe away from my shop door. I have respectable customers, and she drives them away with her constant badgering

"YOU MUST KEEP PHEBE AWAY FROM MY SHOP DOOR."

to tell their fortunes. You know I believe that fortune-telling is wrong, and you are wrong to press your slave into it. You seem intent on destroying my business, and I'll have none of it! If you don't remove her from my shop entry now, I'll be quite justified in reporting you to the magistrates. I've had too many customers complain. Please do something about it right away before she drives more customers away."

Lydia turned on her heels and began to walk resolutely—although she was trembling on the inside—away from Spiro.

It hadn't been easy for Lydia to compete in the business world of male merchants; but when she had been left a widow at the young age of twenty-five, she had determined not to beg but to continue the business of dyeing and selling purple cloth. Her father and husband had taught Lydia the trade. First, they would crush the murex shellfish, cook the crushed shells in saltwater, and then dry them in the sun. That process caused the shells to give off a purple secretion. They further prepared the dyes by mixing water, potash, lime, and the dye. Into this dye mixture would go the yarn. Sometimes, wool from sheep was used. Sometimes linen made from flax would be used. Finally, it would be rinsed in clear water, dried in the sun, and made into the fine cloth that the nobility and wealthy of the city would come to her shop to buy.

Thyatira, her hometown, had had too many folks selling purple, so her family had left and headed for Philippi, where she now had a thriving business. At last, Lydia's hard work had paid off, and she was considered successful even by Roman standards. Now, her success was being threatened because Dimitri and Spiro always sent Phebe to stand by her shop to hawk her fortune-telling powers. Lydia had tried to be kind, even inviting Phebe to a pita bread and cheese lunch while she explained to her why she wasn't welcome outside her shop door. The real problem was with Dimitri and Spiro, for Lydia quickly realized they weren't about to give up a chance to extract a few pennies from the wealthy. Perhaps it would be necessary to call the magistrates. She hoped not.

The looming mountains to the north caught Lydia's attention as she walked back to her shop. Many of the Greeks felt that gods had come from the mountains; and although Lydia still looked to the mountains in awe, her search of the Jewish Scriptures had revealed that there was just one God. He had made the mountains and the earth, and she was to worship Him. She was glad the next day was the Sabbath, and she could go to the riverside with the other worshipers and try to find some peace with God. Lydia still had an emptiness in her heart that even the worship services did not fill. It seemed that all of her life she had searched, but always that void remained.

MOUNTAINS TO THE NORTH CAUGHT LYDIA'S ATTENTION.

2

THE SABBATH

Sun filtered through the tiny window high on the bedroom wall as a gentle breeze stroked Lydia's cheek and stirred her into wakefulness. A knot tightened in her stomach as she recalled the previous day's encounter with Spiro. She must have been dreaming, for it seemed as if he had just been arguing with her. How relieved she was when she remembered that today the shop would be closed and the servants would have the day off because it was the Sabbath.

LYDIA FOUND HERSELF OUTSIDE THE CITY GATES.

Within an hour, Lydia found herself outside the city gates with little Nicolai holding tightly to her hand. Alexander dashed back and forth between them and some stones that demanded to be picked up and directed at an unknown target. She loved these special times when she could get away from the bustling city to find peace in the quiet of the countryside. Dew still remained on the sparse grass and moistened Lydia's sandaled feet. Three-year-old Nicolai didn't mind the dew at all, and Alexander seemed to go out of his way to get his feet wet.

Stalks of golden winter barley bowed their bearded heads in the morning breeze as if the passing trio were royalty. And indeed, Lydia did feel blessed. She passed a little one-room home; the bare earth often served as a floor for the family cramped inside. A toddler waved shyly from the open door, and Lydia waved back. She had often been tempted to invite them to the services; but knowing they were not Jewish or even a Jewish proselyte as she was, she felt they would not be interested. Instead, she kept up her ritual of waving each week as she passed by their home.

This was a glorious morning, and she was not going to allow thoughts of Spiro and Dimitri to spoil it. They might have plans to ruin her business, but she was determined not to let them get the best of her.

To her left, past the willow trees, the Gangites River came into view in all its rugged splendor. Rocks split the water and threw it into a myriad of miniature white fountains and waterfalls. The rushing of the water drew Lydia into a sense of wonder. Surely, if God was anywhere, He was in this place.

She could see other women and their children already gathered at the meeting place quietly praying. Folding her Chilton gracefully around her, Lydia lowered herself to a rock and motioned to Nicolai to sit quietly by her side. Alexander already sat with head bowed. The women had no one to speak to them since there were no men in their group to take that position, but Lydia felt the presence of God as she went to Him in prayer. Often, they would have a good discussion afterward about God's commands, promises, or prophecies before they dispersed. Lydia found herself hungering for more and more each time she came to the meeting. She had been going to Jewish meetings since she had married a Jewish man. Although he had died, she still felt compelled to go and to teach his sons about the Jewish God. There was so much to learn!

Lydia bowed to pray, but felt a tug at her arm. She was giving Nicolai an it's-time-to-be-quiet-and-behave look but stopped short when he whispered, "Mama, some no-hair men are coming. Let's hide."

"No, no, let's wait and see what they want," Lydia whispered with a reassuring smile.

"Greetings!" The other women were now staring in the direction of the three strangers as the oldest of the three stepped forward and introduced himself as Paul from Tarsus and his friends

"GREETINGS!"

Silas and Luke. He surprised the women by asking if he could join the group and speak to them.

"Please do," Lydia quickly invited.

Paul rolled the scroll to Isaiah 53.

" 'Who hath believed our report? and to whom is the arm of the LORD revealed? For he shall grow up before him as a tender plant, and as a root out of a dry ground: he hath no form nor comeliness; and when we shall see him, there is no beauty that we should desire him. He is despised and rejected of men; a man of sorrows, and acquainted with grief: and we hid as it were our faces from him; he was despised, and we esteemed him not. Surely he hath borne our griefs, and carried our sorrows: yet we did esteem him stricken, smitten of God, and afflicted. But he was wounded for our transgressions, he was bruised for our iniquities: the chastisement of our peace was upon him; and with his stripes we are healed. All we like sheep have gone astray; we have turned every one to his own way; and the LORD hath laid on him the iniquity of us

"HE IS DESPISED AND REJECTED, THIS LAMB OF GOD."

all. He was oppressed, and he was afflicted, yet he opened not his mouth: he is brought as a lamb to the slaughter, and as a sheep before her shearers is dumb, so he openeth not his mouth. He was taken from prison and from judgment: and who shall declare his generation? for he was cut off out of the land of the living: for the transgression of my people was he stricken. And he made his grave with the wicked, and with the rich in his death; because he had done no violence, neither was any deceit in his mouth. Yet it pleased the LORD to bruise him; he hath put him to grief: when thou shalt make his soul an offering for sin, he shall see his seed, he shall prolong his days, and the pleasure of the LORD shall prosper in his hand. He shall see of the travail of his soul, and shall be satisfied: by his knowledge shall my righteous servant justify many; for he shall bear their iniquities. Therefore will I divide him a portion with the great, and he shall divide the spoil with the strong; because he hath poured out his soul unto death: and he was numbered with

"...AND THE LORD HATH LAID ON HIM
THE INIQUITY OF US ALL."

the transgressors; and he bare the sin of many, and made intercession for the transgressors.' "

He had Lydia hooked. She couldn't remember ever hearing this Scripture taught before.

"I am one who despised and rejected this lamb of God," Paul proclaimed. "I persecuted His followers; but He loved me in spite of all I had done, and He saved me from all my sins, which separated me from God. I was on my way to Damascus to kill or imprison Christ's followers when the Lord appeared to me and said, 'Saul, Saul, why persecutest thou Me?' When I questioned who it was that spoke, He answered, 'I am Jesus whom thou persecutest: it is hard for thee to kick against the pricks.' For three days, I was left totally blind; but when Ananias, one of the Christian leaders at Damascus, ministered to me, I was healed by Jesus' power and my sight was restored. This man Jesus is truly the Messiah for whom you look."

Paul then told the group that Jesus was born in a stable, born to a virgin, lived a sinless life, was

"SAUL, SAUL, WHY PERSECUTEST THOU ME?"

crucified and buried, then rose from the grave within three days. He said that this Jesus later ascended into heaven. All of this was accomplished according to the Scripture that he had read to them.

Lydia hung on every word the stranger called Paul said. Paul's message was it! This teaching about the Messiah was what was missing and what left that emptiness in her heart. She needed the same salvation that Paul needed. The Jewish Messiah had come! And, according to Paul's words, Jesus could do as much for the Gentiles as He had done for the Jews.

As Paul, Silas, and Luke were about to go, Lydia slipped over to Paul and quietly asked, "What can I do to have the salvation you have?"

"Do you believe Jesus is the Messiah—the Savior?" asked Paul.

"I'm certain of it. I know He spoke to my heart just now," Lydia responded.

"Then ask Him to forgive you of your sins and invite Him into your heart as your Savior right

"WHAT CAN I DO TO HAVE THE SALVATION YOU HAVE?"

now," directed Paul. Lydia immediately bowed before the strangers and all the women and fervently prayed for God's forgiveness. By faith, she knew Jesus was her Savior, and she asked Him into her heart. The emptiness vanished, and so did the knot in her stomach. An overwhelming peace flooded her soul.

She was surprised to see Silas talking to Alexander and realized that he, too, must have felt the same drawing to Christ that she had felt.

"I baptize you in the name of the Father, and of the Son, and of the Holy Ghost." Lydia felt her body going under the sparkling, gurgling water as Paul continued, "buried in the likeness of His death and raised in the likeness of His resurrection." With help from Silas, she made her way to the bank and watched as her son was baptized. It all seemed so marvelous as she hugged her young son, the newborn Christian.

As Paul and Silas came out of the river, Lydia hurried to them. "Please, if you believe I am faithful to the Lord, come to my house and stay with us while you minister in Philippi," Lydia invited.

"I'm afraid you'd find the three of us to be quite a burden on your family. We can find an inn to stay in while we're here," Silas replied.

"You would be no burden. We have plenty of room, and I have servants to help in preparing our meals. Please come. I have so many questions to ask, and I do want my father to meet you," Lydia pleaded.

Paul looked at Silas and Luke and shrugged. "I don't think we can find a better offer. Perhaps we can be of some help to your family."

"You already have been," Lydia said.

"COME, COME. HERE IN MY COURTYARD. . ."

3

THE HOUSE CHURCH

"Come, come. Here in my courtyard—sit and dine with me," old, bent-over Grandfather invited as he gingerly led Paul, Silas, and Luke into a huge courtyard of Lydia's home. Lydia had introduced them and gone to the kitchen to give the servants instructions on fixing a meal and preparing rooms for the visitors.

A stylish, graceful-looking chair beckoned to Paul to come and rest his weary feet. "Thank you," he replied. "It's been a long walk for these old feet."

"Oh, I'm sorry about the rock floor," Grandfather apologized as the three looked at one another in bewilderment. "We have so many stones and rocks around here that we feel we have to use them somewhere."

Then they realized Grandfather was hard of hearing and had confused rock with walk. Paul wondered what else Grandfather thought he'd said.

"We have so many rocks in this land they say that when the gods made the earth, a big sieve separated the good soil from the rocks, and when they were finished, they dumped all the rocks in this land!" Grandfather chuckled as he shared the story he had told so many times before to anyone who would listen.

Paul spoke louder now. "We have come to share the good news of the one true God who has provided the way of salvation."

"Zeus god? Oh, yes! He is very powerful.

He rules all the sky and all the earth," cut in Grandfather.

Paul tried to talk even louder now. "Your daughter accepted Jesus, the one true God, today."

"My daughter's God?" Grandfather shook his head. "She follows the God of the Jews. I cannot keep all of His laws. They have many scrolls with laws. No, this old man will have to stay with the gods of his people. Perhaps they will smile upon me. I will have to take my chances with them."

Luke and Silas looked hopelessly at Paul. He was not making any progress with this conversation.

Gabe, the servant, came with the meal; Lydia and her boys soon followed. Lydia's friend, Elizabeth, explained that she had told her husband of the morning's events at the river, and now they both wanted to hear more of what Paul and his companions had to say. Lydia found that this scene was played over several times in the next few days. Finally, she went to Silas with her scheme.

"Why not start a church here in my home?" she

"WHY NOT START A CHURCH HERE?"

questioned. "The courtyard is big enough to seat plenty of people. We could meet here every Sabbath. All of us could invite our friends and acquaintances." Bubbling over with ideas, Lydia could hardly contain herself. Oh, how she wanted to know of Jesus!

Soon, arrangements were settled, and everyone went to work. Lydia and Alexander invited many who came to the shop. Some immediately turned them down. They were not interested in this new sect. Others were curious, and a few came close to promising to come. Joy flooded through Lydia when she was able to talk to someone about Jesus.

As the Sabbath day approached, the family in the one-room house began to possess Lydia's thoughts. Should she invite them? All the others who had been invited were from well-to-do families. The country family would probably feel out of place, she reasoned. But something wouldn't let her rest with that decision, and off she went again with little Nicolai. Alexander was left to tend the shop.

As Lydia walked the pathway to the front door, the little girl who always waved to them on the Sabbath slipped back inside the house. Lydia could hear her calling for her mother.

"Hello, I'm Lydia. I've passed by often on my way to prayer meeting. Now we are having a special service at my house. Paul, an apostle of Jesus Christ, has good news about God for all of us—even us Gentiles, as we are called by our Jewish friends. I would like you and your family to come," Lydia invited.

"Oh, we couldn't," the mother protested. "We would not be accepted by those ladies. Our clothes are too old, and we have no sandals to wear."

"But our God looks at the heart," Lydia reassured her. "The services are at my house. Here are the directions. I'd love to have you come. Please come and sit with my family and me." Suddenly, Lydia realized she wanted this young mother there more than she wanted anyone else. "Please come."

"WE HAVE NO SANDALS TO WEAR."

"I'll try," the young mother promised shyly.

"Wonderful! I'll have Gabe look for you. By the way, what is your name?"

"Secunda," came a timid reply.

Her heart light, Lydia sang all the way back to Philippi.

Quite a group was gathering on the balcony and in the courtyard, but Lydia still hadn't spotted Secunda when the worship service was about to begin. Paul, Silas, and Luke were still in their room praying. Then, at the entrance, she saw Gabe motioning for her and caught sight of some children close by. She flew down the stairway and went straight to Secunda. "Welcome, welcome. I'm glad you're here."

Secunda couldn't help but feel wanted with Lydia there. Lydia led Secunda and her three young children up the stairway and to the balcony just as Paul was about to begin.

Every word Paul said was taken in by Lydia.

"IF ONLY HE COULD READ."

She noticed how carefully Secunda listened, too. "Could this possibly be true?" Secunda asked. "It seems too good to be possible."

"Very true," Lydia responded confidently.

"I don't understand it all. May I come back for another service?" questioned Secunda.

"Certainly, come every week. Come any time. We'll help in whatever way we can," Lydia responded as Secunda made her way through the door and into the busy Philippian street.

What a day it had been! Ten had believed in Jesus. Grandfather had come, but he only caught bits and pieces so he had no idea what was going on.

"If only he could read," Luke lamented.

"But he can!" exclaimed Lydia.

"That's it!" exulted Luke. "I'll just write all I know about Jesus, and I'll take notes on Paul's preaching. Something should make the gospel clear to him."

Lydia felt so much better now knowing that Grandfather would receive the message of the gospel. If only her husband had not died, he could have heard the gospel, too. How sad that it was too late for him!

"THESE MEN ARE SERVANTS OF THE MOST HIGH GOD. . . ."

4

THE SLAVE GIRL

"Jesus, the Son of God, gave His life—"

"These men are servants of the most high God, which show unto us the way of salvation," the girl cut in.

Paul continued. "The Son of God gave His life so that you might live eter—"

"These men are the servants of the most high God, which show unto us the way of salvation," came the cry from Phebe again as a ripple of laughter ran through the crowd.

To say the least, Paul was frustrated. What the slave girl said was true; but every day, as he tried to tell anyone the wonderful news about Jesus, this girl called Phebe kept interrupting with her divinations. As the crowd dispersed in different directions, Paul had to admit that it was obvious that he had lost this gathering for now.

The men decided to make their way back to their room at Lydia's. Luke was eager to talk to Grandfather anyway. He was thrilled that Grandfather was reading his account of the life and death of Jesus, and he wanted to be there to answer any questions the old man might have. Sure enough, Grandfather had questions; and by talking extremely loud, using hand motions, and writing some things that were impossible to get across any other way, Luke was able to help Grandfather understand.

The entire household was overjoyed when Grandfather finally announced, "I believe the message about Jesus! I believe it! Young man, I believe it!"

Paul was happy, but he was still burdened about Phebe. So many people in Philippi were open to his message, but the devil was using the poor slave girl to interrupt everything he said. He could not eat that evening, and the next morning he spent fasting and praying.

Lydia was concerned for Paul. She knew how persistent Phebe could be. Lydia also understood the power and wealth of Spiro and Dimitri. She offered Paul more food that the servants had prepared, but he politely refused. "I'm going to try again. Pray for us," he pleaded as he went to get Luke and Silas.

A crowd was just starting to gather around Paul when he heard it again. "These men are—"

Paul turned in the direction of the voice and saw Phebe standing there in bare feet and ragged clothes. He looked at her glassy eyes and ordered, "I command thee in the name of Jesus Christ to come out of her."

Instantly, her glassy-eyed look was gone, and Phebe fell down where she had stood and quietly worshiped God.

Paul was free to preach now, and a host of people congregated to hear this new philosophy of life. The people had heard about so many gods before, but this God seemed different—powerful and yet personal.

Word spread quickly about Phebe's deliverance from the evil spirits, and that drew even more people. Silas dealt with those who accepted Jesus as their Messiah.

Just as Paul was about to conclude, two men—one short and plump and the other a tall man with curly, graying hair—pushed their way through the crowd. "Hey, what is the meaning of this? Phebe is our property, and you have no right to cast the spirits from her," Spiro bellowed.

"This is going to cost you a bundle," Dimitri threatened.

"The law may say that she is your property,

"I COMMAND THEE IN THE NAME OF JESUS CHRIST TO COME OUT OF HER."

but she is a child of God now and is free from the control of that evil spirit, and in that, we rejoice," Paul defended.

At that, Dimitri grabbed Paul and Spiro jerked at Silas and pulled them through the mob, which opened the way for the two smooth-talking men. The people knew that Spiro and Dimitri had close connections with powerful people.

As they dragged the two through the marketplace, Alexander watched the action from the shop door and begged his mother to allow him to see what it was all about. When he saw that Paul and Silas were being harassed by Dimitri and Spiro, the poor boy wasn't sure whether to run back and get help or follow the group to see what would happen. Before he could decide, they had Paul and Silas before the magistrates.

"These Jews bring nothing but trouble to Philippi!" Spiro accused.

"Aren't we Romans here?" questioned Dimitri.

"The things that these two teach are not lawful for us to hear or do!"

Suddenly, the mob went wild. They were proud to be a Roman colony with all of the rights of Roman citizenship. They certainly did not want to do anything to jeopardize their rights. Turning against Paul and Silas, they called for punishment.

Alexander cried out, "No! No!" but his lonely protest was lost in the din of the crowd. He ran back for help as the magistrates stripped the prisoners of their clothes and had them beaten with rods until the blood ran down their bodies and trickled onto the rocky pavement.

Alexander's legs couldn't carry him fast enough as he heard the cry go up for their imprisonment.

5

DISASTER AFTER MIDNIGHT

"Alexander, what is wrong?" Lydia cried as her son gasped for breath and tried to say something when he entered the shop.

"They. . .they. . .took them. . .to prison," he forced out.

"Took them? Them who?" Lydia demanded.

"Paul. . .and Silas," Alexander managed as he caught his breath.

Lydia couldn't believe what her son was saying. "Whatever for? They wouldn't break any laws."

"THEY. . .THEY. . .TOOK THEM. . .TO PRISON."

"It was Spiro and Dimitri's doing. They accused them of teaching things that are unlawful for Roman citizens, and that made the mob really angry. I think Spiro and Dimitri are upset because Paul healed Phebe, and they can't make all that money off her and—oh, Mama, they beat them a lot! There won't be anyone to take care of their wounds in prison. We have to do something to help them!" insisted Alexander.

"They didn't take Luke?" Lydia asked.

"He wasn't with them," answered Alexander.

"That's a relief. Go see if you can find Luke. Look for him as you pass through the marketplace, but check at the house first. I'll be there as soon as I can give Lucius instructions for the shop. Now, run on—and, Alexander, don't go near the prison."

Old Lucius's face went white as Lydia explained the situation. He, too, had been in jail when he had first been taken from his home country after his nation had been defeated in battle. Many of his fellow citizens had been brought as slaves to this

LUCIUS'S FACE WENT WHITE. . . .

conquering nation. He had been young and strong, and he'd tried to escape. For that, he had spent several years in jail until his will had been destroyed. Grandfather had rescued him by buying his freedom from the prison, and later Lydia had freed him with all of her other slaves. His loyalty was so great that he stayed with her as her servant, for he did not easily forget the awful damp darkness of that prison from which her family had saved him. "Don't worry about this shop. Old Lucius will keep it going. You run along with Luke and get those two fine men out of that place."

Lydia was grateful to find Luke waiting anxiously in the courtyard when she arrived home. "What can we do? We must do something quickly, or they'll die in that dreadful prison," lamented Lydia.

"Lydia, you're going to have to try to persuade the magistrates to free them," Luke replied evenly. Being a doctor, Luke knew the seriousness of the situation and with urgency, gravely added, "You're the only one to whom they might listen."

Lydia felt the weight of the world coming down upon her. "Oh, God," she prayed, "help me now. I don't know what to do."

Lydia knew the magistrates, but she knew that Spiro and Dimitri had plenty of clout with them, too—and now so many people had turned on Paul and Silas. It would be very difficult to convince the magistrates to free the preachers.

"We must pray first," she declared firmly. "In the morning, I will go. Tonight it is too late to call on the magistrates. Soon they'll be home with their families and will not want their meal to be bothered. Pray that God will give me wisdom and the right words to say when the new day comes."

After making certain that everyone who cared to eat had been served, Lydia took three-year-old Nicolai by the hand, led him to his room, and tucked him into his cozy bed. "Come, Tracker," Nicolai commanded, and the little ball of energy that was his new puppy came bounding from the courtyard and under Lydia's feet. With his round face, dark hair, and big brown eyes, Nicolai looked trustingly into Lydia's eyes and melted her heart. There were so many injustices her little one might have to face. She would have to do what she could to make things right for Paul and Silas if things were ever to be right for Nicolai.

Softly, Lydia sang her son to sleep.

Little child of God,
Go to sleep.
While your mother's love
Doth gently keep
All her little ones
In her care,
For our God above
Has love to share.

She tiptoed from the room and quietly retired to her own room, where she prayed until she heard the sound of flutes and harps and loud

LYDIA SANG HER SON TO SLEEP.

singing as revelers made their way home from disorderly feasts at the home of some overly generous hosts. *Too much Roman influence,* thought Lydia, and then remembered as she thought aloud. "Paul and Silas are Roman citizens. They can't legally be beaten or imprisoned as they have been!" She would use that to persuade the magistrates to free them.

A peaceful sleep had overcome Lydia only to be broken suddenly by a dizzy sensation as she felt the room move. In the moonlight, she could see the candles gently swaying on the bronze candelabrum. A sudden jolt caused her to sit straight up in bed; as the rumbling and shaking continued, she realized it was an earthquake! She jumped to her feet and started for the courtyard just as a thunderous explosion shook the room. Feeling her way through the doorway, she shouted, "Nicolai! Alexander! Grandfather! Luke! Oh, where is everyone?"

"Mother, I'm here." She was relieved to hear

Alexander's excited voice.

Luke came into the courtyard with Grandfather hanging on to him. "Sit here under the open sky." He calmed the excited old man.

Then, standing in the moonlight, Lydia gave a sharp cry. She knew what had caused the explosion. "Nicolai! Oh, Nicolai's room! The balcony has fallen and trapped him in his room. We must get him out! There could be another tremor that might bring down the whole house!"

She hurried over to the pile of debris and called, "Nicolai, can you hear me?"

"Mama, my door's shut, and I can't get out," Nicolai whimpered.

Lydia breathed a sigh of relief. "Nicolai, are there any holes in the wall?"

"No, Mama. Tracker and I looked, and we're stuck in here. Mama, Tracker is really scared. Would you please hurry and get us out?" he pleaded as another slight tremor shook the ground under the group in the courtyard.

"NICOLAI, CAN YOU HEAR ME?"

Faithful Gabe stepped forward and offered, "There is a way to get him out, but we'll have to be very careful or the whole ceiling and wall might cave in. First, we need to get as much rubble out of the way as we can, but be very careful not to move anything that might be supporting the ceiling or wall. When we get as far back as the wall, we can shore it up with the bed frames."

"I'll get mine," Luke volunteered even though he knew it was still dangerous to go back inside the building.

"Nicolai, you must be patient now," Lydia said. "We are starting to dig you out, but it'll take some time."

"Oh, Mama, I'm glad you came. You'll get me out 'cause you love me. Tracker doesn't understand that, so please hurry, or he'll get really scared," begged Nicolai.

Everyone was busy throwing broken clay and pieces of wood and bricks into the open courtyard as Lydia kept talking to the frightened boy.

Wood was cut in small pieces to make a frame for a tunnel that would lead back through the caved-in door. "I hear a puppy scratching," Gabe shouted jubilantly. "We're almost there!"

Everyone held his breath and prayed that there would be no more severe tremors until the boy was safely out of the trap.

As another tremor shook the earth, Gabe said, "Everyone stay in the open courtyard. There's no need to have everyone trapped if this wall gives out."

He was digging carefully until Lydia noticed that it was quiet and no more brick fragments were being thrown from the tunnel. "Let this be it," she prayed.

"I've got him!" Gabe shouted and soon had the boy pulled to safety. Tracker came bounding behind him, jumping up and down, licking everyone who allowed it, and greeting them all with an excited yelp.

"Mama, Tracker and I didn't break the wall. It

WOOD WAS CUT. . .TO MAKE A FRAME FOR A TUNNEL.

just broke by itself," Nicolai declared defensively.

"I know," Lydia reassured him. "It was an earthquake." The servant girl had already brought blankets, and Lydia wrapped Nicolai tightly in one and sang her lullaby once again to him. Alexander snuggled in next to Nicolai. Even though the earth continued to tremble, they felt safe and thankful under the great ceiling of God's starry sky. Sleep came quickly. Dawn would not wait long.

"MAMA, TRACKER AND I DIDN'T BREAK THE WALL."

6

Unexpected Visitors

A sharp rap on the door brought Lydia immediately out of her peaceful sleep. Any noise reminded the sleeping group of the previous night's harrowing experience with the devastating earthquake. Gabe was the first to reach the door, and he was soon back announcing, "An answer to our prayers," as he led Paul and Silas into the courtyard.

Paul noticed the fallen balcony and quickly scanned the room until he spotted Nicolai with Alexander and Tracker close beside him. He looked

"AN ANSWER TO OUR PRAYERS."

obviously relieved.

"How did you get free?" Lydia inquired.

"God works in strange and miraculous ways. You might find this hard to believe, but we're not the only ones God set free today," Paul declared as he began his story of their unusual deliverance.

"When they took us to prison, they gave the jailer very strict orders to make sure we didn't escape. In order to ensure that we couldn't flee, he led us past the other prisoners in that damp, dark, cave-like hold and to the inner prison. As if that wasn't enough, he put our feet in stocks. Then, knowing there was no earthly way we could free ourselves—especially in our condition—he settled back for an easy evening. Well, I just looked at Silas, and we both knew what we were going to do. We had a captive audience and intended to serve the Lord right where we were! I prayed awhile, and then Silas did, and we just thanked and praised God for everything—even being in jail. Then we started singing. God be praised! He gave us a song in our hearts

"THE EARTHQUAKE!" ALEXANDER SHOUTED.

even in the musty staleness of that jail. You can guess what happened next."

"The earthquake!" Alexander shouted.

"You're right," Paul responded. "And it shook the foundation of that prison so hard that all the doors opened and everyone's shackles were broken loose."

"And you all escaped!" Alexander cut in.

"Not exactly. God still wanted us there," Paul continued. "Of course, the earthquake woke the jailer; and when he realized what had happened, he figured all the prisoners were gone, and he pulled his sword from its sheath and was going to kill himself with his own sword rather than suffer a worse fate at the hands of the Romans. I realized what was happening and cried, 'Do thyself no harm: for we are all here.'

"My heart went out to him as he came in carrying a torch light, and I could see that he was trembling all over. He took us out of there and asked, 'Sirs, what must I do to be saved?'

HE ASKED IF HE COULD BE BAPTIZED.

"We explained that he had to believe on the Lord Jesus Christ, and we preached the gospel to him and to all the members of his household.

"By that time, our oozing wounds were starting to stick to our torn clothing, which was also encrusted with dirt from the streets and prison. It was just a matter of time before infection would have made our physical conditions even more miserable. But that Philippian jailer carefully and graciously cleaned those ugly wounds. No sooner had he finished cleaning our wounds than he asked if he could be baptized. So we baptized him and all of the others in his family. What a wonderful time of rejoicing we had while the rest of the city cleaned the mess left by the earthquake! The jailer even had a sumptuous meal prepared for us.

"Now, this morning the magistrates sent a message with the sergeants to let us go. I don't know if they took the earthquake as a bad omen, but the jailer came and told us to go in peace. But I thought of our testimony and how we, along with the cause

"WE MUST LEAVE THE CITY NOW."

of Christ, had been disgraced publicly. I told them that we, as Roman citizens, had been publicly beaten before we were tried and found guilty. There was no way they were going just quietly to release us. I insisted that the magistrates themselves come and release us. When they heard that we were Roman citizens, they feared what might happen to them, so they came personally and freed us. They asked us to leave the city because they were afraid of what trouble might come to them if their superiors discovered what they had done. So you see, God used the earthquake not only to free us, but also to free the jailer and all his family.

"We must leave this city now. Thessalonica should be our next stop. Remember how God has blessed and worked so many miracles. Let this always be a comfort and encouragement to you when Satan tries to turn you from our Lord. I'll write to you and try to return. May God's peace keep you no matter what comes your way."

Tears welled up in Lydia's eyes as the men of

God made their way through the door and down the dusty street. They were tears of joy. Her life was so full.

7

THE PHILIPPIAN JAILER

Most of the rubble had been removed from the courtyard, although the balcony had not yet been replaced. It had been decided that services would be held as usual on the Lord's Day. Lydia had just settled in beside Secunda when a stir at the doorway drew her attention away from the young Christian man who was about to speak. It was the jailer and his family! They had arrived just in time for the services, and Luke helped them quickly find seats. Lydia noticed they all listened intently as the speaker

"I'D LIKE TO APOLOGIZE FOR ANY PROBLEMS YOU EXPERIENCED. . . ."

testified about what Christ had done for him.

After services, the jailer approached Lydia. "I'd like to apologize for any problems you experienced as a result of Paul and Silas's imprisonment. Certainly, Spiro and Dimitri intended for evil to come of it, but God has brought a great blessing, too. I notice you have some severe structural damage from the quake. I'd be glad to bring my sons to help restore your balcony."

"We would appreciate the help," Lydia said as she thanked him.

"What I'd most like, though, is to be able to tell these people what happened to me and how God led me here."

Lydia beamed. "I've heard from Paul about that night. It would be wonderful to hear your testimony at the very next—" Lydia cut herself short. "Oh, look! Phebe is here. Excuse me!"

She hurried over to where Phebe stood timidly in the shadows. A frightened look covered her face, and she was obviously trembling.

"OH, LYDIA, YOU HAVE BEEN SO PATIENT WITH ME. . . ."

"Why, Phebe, what is wrong?" asked Lydia. "This is such a joyous occasion when you think of all God has done and realize how He protected us during the earthquake. Are you still frightened by the earthquake?"

"Oh, Lydia, you have been so patient with me, and I've caused you so many problems; but now, I'm really in trouble. You see, I've run away from my masters, and if they find me—especially here—I know I'll be beaten severely; but I just had to come today. How can I escape from them? Oh, Lydia, please help me," cried Phebe.

Concern showing on her face, the jailer's wife made her way from the doorway to Phebe and Lydia. "Quickly, you must get out. Spiro is at the front door talking to my husband. They are looking for you, Phebe," she whispered.

"This way, Phebe, hurry," directed Lydia.

She took the young girl by the hand and practically dragged her from the courtyard, through several other rooms, and into the storeroom where

"SPIRO IS AT THE FRONT DOOR
TALKING TO MY HUSBAND."

pottery jars full of oil, grain, fruit, and vegetables were stored. "There is a door here to the back street. Run swiftly to Spiro's house. There, continue your work as usual. Tomorrow, I'll send an acquaintance with money to buy you. Do not let them know that I am the one buying you from them, or they may not sell. Since you no longer possess the powers of divination, your value to them has greatly diminished. They may be eager to sell you. Pray that they will be willing. Now hurry, and try to get back before they do. May God go with you."

The shaking girl gave Lydia a grateful look and dashed off through the street.

Lydia smoothed her Chilton and slowly made her way back to the courtyard, where she overheard Spiro's voice coming from the street. "You really do need to think about what this is going to do to you in this city. How do you expect to advance if you're going to be seen associating with this Christian sect—and so many of them are Jews. Why, you know all of the Jews have been banished

**"THIS IS MUCH TOO IMPORTANT FOR ME
TO GIVE UP THAT EASILY."**

from Rome. You'll be put at the bottom of the list for any promotions."

"This is much too important for me to give up that easily. You see, Jesus died for me. The least I can do is sacrifice a promotion," came the reply.

"But it could even cost you your job as a jailer. Then what would your family do? I tell you as my friend, you'd better stay away from this place. There are plenty of gods to worship in our own culture," Spiro continued.

"As a friend, I must tell you that this Jesus is very different from the gods that we have worshiped for so many years. He is the true God and has real power both to care for us in this life and to keep us in a life after death. I've witnessed the miracles that He works! I could not turn my back on Him now. Spiro, you need to consider—"

"Oh, no, don't try to include me in this foolishness," cut in Spiro as he got the idea of what the jailer was trying to say. "I was just trying to help you and your family. I've been around for awhile, you

"DON'T TRY TO INCLUDE ME IN THIS FOOLISHNESS."

know, and I know how these things work; but if you're not willing to listen, you'll have to work out your own problems. I'll be on my way now. That girl is more trouble than she's worth—especially since Paul ruined her. It's going to take a lot of stripes to retrain her to make her worth anything to me now," Spiro scoffed as he stormed away.

"What was that all about?" Lydia questioned.

The jailer shook his head. "I'm not quite sure, but I don't think we've heard the last from that one."

"I DON'T THINK WE'VE HEARD THE LAST FROM THAT ONE."

8

COMPETITION

As Lydia entered the sales room through the curtained doorway, Phebe motioned her to the open door that led to the street of the fabric merchants. Directly across the street, one of Lydia's valued customers entered the newly opened shop of Dimitri and Spiro.

"He was ready to enter our shop when Dimitri came along and started chatting with him," Phebe explained. "The first thing you know, he was telling him of their new shop and said the prices were

"HE'S TAKEN ANOTHER CUSTOMER!"

much better than ours—and now look—he's taken another customer!"

Lydia breathed a deep sign of exasperation. It seemed that Spiro and Dimitri would never give up their quest to destroy her. It had been ten years since that day when she had made arrangements to buy Phebe from the two. She had given Phebe her freedom; but having nowhere to go, Phebe had chosen to stay and work for Lydia. She had proved to be a tremendous help both in the shop and at home, as she was totally devoted to Lydia, knowing that Lydia had paid the price for her freedom. Lydia looked with admiration upon the beautiful young girl, for she was strong and yet ladylike. A daughter of her own could not have meant any more to Lydia than Phebe meant.

Now Phebe worried. "It's all my fault. They wouldn't be doing this to you if you hadn't saved my life. Their hearts are very hard to all that is good. Money is everything to them."

"Don't you be blaming yourself," Lydia reassured

her. "It's a most wonderful miracle that God rid you of the powers of divination; and if I lose everything, I'll not regret that or buying your freedom. But who would have guessed that Jason, the richest philosopher in Philippi, would have ever backed them in a business venture? It's still a shock to me that they've gone into the business of dyeing purple cloth. Of course, they can see that we have profited from it, but it's taken many years and plenty of hard work."

"Lydia, why do you suppose Jason would back them in the first place?" asked Phebe.

"I've heard that he has very strong ideas about the goodness—perhaps even a godliness—that is in all men. He doesn't like it that Jews and Christians teach that our righteousness is as filthy rags, and Christians teach that we need Jesus to save us from our sins. He has been working hard to stop the spread of Christianity. Since the church meets at my home, it would serve his purposes well if Spiro and Dimitri could destroy my business and cause

"WHY DO YOU SUPPOSE JASON WOULD BACK THEM?"

me to lose my home, thus giving the church no place to meet."

"How did Jason get to be so wealthy?" Phebe questioned.

"His family has been in Philippi for many years," Lydia replied. "Before the mines were over-quarried, his family owned a number of gold mines in the hills that surround Philippi. The wealth has been passed down from generation to generation, and Jason has invested wisely. I'm afraid with that, Jason has developed a great sense of pride in his wealth and all that he has been able to accomplish with that wealth. He has no interest in a Savior, for he sees no need of a Savior for a man like himself. Pride can be a dangerous thing, Phebe. Remember, any good we possess or any good we may accomplish comes only through God's grace. Only through Him can we have righteousness."

Their conversation was shortened by the appearance of a long-standing customer. "Glad to see you're still in business," he said with a twinkle in his eye. "I've been over checking out the competition. They certainly tried to sell me on their purple cloth, but I'm a little wiser than they figured," he said.

"What do you mean?" questioned Lydia.

"I've been buying from you for years now, Lydia, and I know you have quality merchandise. I've had a little experience in weaving, too. All I had to do was look carefully at their cloth, and I knew anyone buying from them would be cheated—even though they're selling at a much cheaper price. You see how finely woven your cloth is?" he questioned as he stretched out a piece of material on the counter. "Well, their material does not have nearly as many threads per span. I wouldn't think anyone would waste purple dye on such poor quality material; but enough people wouldn't notice, and Spiro and Dimitri aren't above cheating people if they think they can get away with it. It won't work with me, though," he firmly declared.

"GLAD TO SEE YOU'RE STILL IN BUSINESS."

"YOU SEE HOW FINELY WOVEN YOUR CLOTH IS?"

"I'm certainly glad you find our cloth of high quality," Lydia said. "I wondered how they could undersell us by so much and still realize a profit. The only problem is, most of my customers won't recognize the difference until it's too late to do anything about it."

"Be assured, I won't keep it a secret that this is the better buy. I hope that will help you some," the satisfied customer replied.

"No doubt, that will help. Thank you so much," came Lydia's response.

"I just hope it helps enough," Phebe said when the man had made his way back to the street of the fabric merchants.

Catching a glimpse of Dimitri leaving his shop, Lydia went to meet him. "What is your purpose in underselling me with cheap material?" she challenged.

"Oh, my, we're getting a little feisty now, aren't we?" came Dimitri's snide remark. "I think we can let the people decide which cloth they prefer."

"WE'RE GETTING A LITTLE FEISTY NOW, AREN'T WE?"

"Destroying me at the people's expense will bring you no glory, Dimitri," Lydia proclaimed.

"Now, I'll not cheat anyone," Dimitri said. "And as far as destroying you goes—you didn't feel too badly when our livelihood was destroyed when Phebe lost her divining powers, did you?"

"Dimitri, would you really want Phebe again to be what she was then? Then, she had no control over herself; and now she is a kind, considerate young lady. The change is worth it to me even if I lose my shop and my home!" proclaimed Lydia.

"ALEXANDER MUST GO WITH YOU—AND DO BEHAVE!"

9

A SPECIAL OFFERING

"Please, Mother," pleaded Nicolai. "It's so exciting when new soldiers come to the city. Please let me go see them!"

Lydia smiled down at her eager son. He was having a very hard time containing the excitement that bubbled out of him. "Alexander must go with you—and do behave!"

Nicolai scrambled from behind the counter and hurried off in search of Alexander. "Alexander, the Roman soldiers are coming on the Egnatia Highway.

Hurry, let's go!" he shouted when he spotted his older brother. Off the two went through the crowded market streets. Nicolai could hear the steady rhythm of the soldiers' feet marching with an unvarying beat as they moved through the throngs of people.

Soon, he pointed with enthusiasm at the moving sea of red himations that each soldier had slung properly over his shoulder. Under that, they wore short woolen Chiltons covered by a leather breastplate with metal disks sewn on them to protect their chests. Their black boots were laced high and greaves were fastened around their legs. Each soldier was crowned with a metal helmet topped by a crest of horsehair. They all carried swords and daggers so that no intelligent person would test their authority.

The whole scene made such an impression on Nicolai that he was proud to be a part of the Roman colony. Looking up at Alexander, he asked, "Aren't you glad we were born as Roman citizens?"

"Yes," Alexander replied. "I wouldn't want to be on the wrong side of those guys."

As always, merchants and traders, preachers and pilgrims, messengers, and other travelers journeyed with the Roman soldiers in order to assure their own safety from thieves or wild animals as they made their way across the roads the Romans had so masterfully engineered.

Nicolai spotted an old friend pointing in their direction as he spoke to one of the travelers. Grabbing Alexander by the hand, he headed towards the strangers. "Are you the sons of Lydia, the seller of purple?" the stranger asked.

"Yes, sir, we are," Alexander replied politely. "What may we do for you?"

"I would like you to lead me to Lydia's shop. I have a message for her," the stranger answered.

Lydia was visibly shaken when she looked up after reading the message.

"What is it, Mama? What is wrong?" inquired Nicolai.

"It's Paul. You've heard us speak often of our

"PAUL IS A PRISONER. . .IN ROME."

missionary friend, and I'm sure Alexander can remember him."

"Oh, yes. How frightening it was when he and Silas were carried off to prison, and then we had that horrible earthquake!" Alexander returned.

"I'm afraid Paul is a prisoner again. This time it is in Rome," Lydia informed them. "He is under house arrest."

"What does that mean, Mama?" Nicolai wanted to know.

"It means that he may live in his own house, but will be chained to a Roman guard. He sounds as though he is happy to be in this predicament so that he can tell the Roman guards about Christ!"

"Perhaps there is nothing to be concerned about then, Mother," Nicolai offered.

"I see a very serious problem," Lydia replied. "If he lives in the house, he must pay some rent. In order to pay the rent, he must work as a tentmaker; but he cannot do that as long as he is chained to the Roman guard! We must do something to help him so he can continue his work with the Roman people."

"Mother," replied Alexander, "we need to take this problem to the church. You know they would want to help. Think of how willing they were to send offerings to Paul when he was in Thessalonica."

Lydia thought for a moment. "Yes, you are right. The church has always been so generous. We'll let the church leaders know, and they should be able to take up a special offering at the next service."

Lydia knew everyone would be liberal with their giving to the ministry, but what could she do? Obviously, in the past, she had been in a position to give more than others in the congregation; but now, with Dimitri and Spiro threatening her livelihood, she had no security for the future. Perhaps it would be best if she did not give this time since that could put her home in jeopardy and they needed her home to serve as the church. Why did this have to happen at such an inopportune time?

"HOW MUCH WILL WE GIVE?"

She knew from her study of the Scripture that she should put the Lord's work first, but which work?

Breaking in on her thoughts, Nicolai asked, "Mama, how much will we give?"

"I don't know, Nicolai. Pray to God. We must get an answer from Him," Lydia answered.

It was agreed that Epaphrodites should take the offering to Paul, and he was happy to volunteer.

In the service, Paul's former companion, Luke, stood and quoted from the Lord Himself.

" 'Give, and it shall be given unto you; good measure, pressed down, and shaken together, and running over, shall men give into your bosom. For with the same measure that ye mete withal it shall be measured to you again' " (Luke 6:38).

No more prayer was needed. Lydia's dilemma was solved. She would give. She would give very generously.

" 'GIVE, AND IT SHALL BE GIVEN UNTO YOU. . . .' "

"I HAVE SOMETHING FOR YOU, MOTHER."

10

FARM IN THE FOOTHILLS

Doing a little hop as he entered the courtyard, Nicolai swung himself in front of Lydia and stood, hands behind his back, wearing a crooked smile. "I have something for you, Mother. Can you guess what it is?"

"Mmm...," Lydia thought out loud. "Could it be a frog?"

"No, Mother. I know you don't like frogs. Guess again," he insisted.

"Perhaps a butterfly—did you catch a pretty

butterfly, Nicolai?" she asked.

"No, Mother, but I did try to catch one this morning," Nicolai informed her. "Just one more guess."

"What could it be?" Lydia wondered as she played along with his game. "I know. It's a stone, right?"

"Wrong."

"Oh, no, it's not a snake, is it?" she asked, taking a step backwards.

Nicolai swung his outstretched right arm directly in front of Lydia. She could smell the sweet aroma of the brilliant yellow rose as Nicolai lifted it to her face.

"For me?" Lydia asked.

Nicolai nodded.

"Oh, it's so beautiful!" Lydia exclaimed as she inhaled the lovely fragrance of the elegant bloom. The flower reminded her that tomorrow would begin the Greater Dionysia, and all the people would wear crowns of blossoms and scatter the petals of

"FOR ME?"

spring everywhere. This festival was also the time the people honored Dionysius, who was also known as Bacchus, the wine god, and drank wine excessively. Lydia quickly made plans to be out of the city for the next few days.

"How would you like to go to the farm tomorrow, Nicolai?" she asked.

"Would I ever! My favorite place!" Nicolai shouted. "Hooray! May we go right now?"

Lydia didn't know who was more excited about going to the farm—Nicolai or Grandfather. Although he had resisted, the family had convinced Grandfather to ride the horse instead of walk to the farm. Now, Alexander led the horse as they neared the farm. Grandfather sat tall, as though he were king of the world, and gave directions to everyone—including the workers who ran to meet them. "Take her to the stable, Son. Be sure Queen is fed and watered, but don't let her drink too much water, and be sure she gets her hay before she gets any

GRANDFATHER SAT TALL, AS THOUGH HE WERE
KING OF THE WORLD. . . .

grain," he commanded loudly.

Of course, the young man knew all of this already; but with a smile, he said, "Yes, sir," and dutifully hustled off to obey.

Lydia and Grandfather spent a relaxing day checking on all the farm workers and the progress that had been made for the spring.

Nicolai headed straight for his old friend, Justin, and begged to be taken hunting.

"Don't forget, it's spring on the farm." Justin chuckled. "Hunting sounds like a nice break, but there's too much work to do to get all the crops planted to even think about going out hunting."

"I'll help!" Nicolai volunteered. "I'll get the ox team ready. Come on, Alexander. You can help, too, then we'll all go hunting." It was such a pleasant and invigorating break from the shop in the city. Alexander helped get the team ready to plow and then made his way to the lower vineyards. There, he worked to cut off the lower branches of the oak and maple trees to keep the grapevines off the ground

"WHY MUST THE SOIL BE TURNED OVER?"

and force them to climb higher in the trees. The pointed stakes were already in place for the vineyards on the upper terraces.

Nicolai walked alongside Justin while he skillfully plowed furrow after furrow of stony earth. The boy took a deep breath. It seemed a strange thing, but he actually enjoyed the smell of the fresh dirt! It was his job to gather any rocks that worked their way to the top in the process of plowing. These he would haul to the edge of the field, where they would later be used to build stone walls and steps.

Thus Nicolai was kept occupied while he waited for Justin to keep his promise of a hunting trip. As questions popped into his head, Nicolai was certain to verbalize them. "Why must the soil be turned over?" he questioned. "Why don't we just poke a hole in the ground and stick a seed in it? That would be much faster, and we could go hunting twice as soon."

"Ah, but if we did not plow the earth, the soil would be very hard, the roots could not spread and acquire the nutrients the plants need. Then all of our plants would be sickly or dead, and we would have little to show for our work of poking them into the ground," Justin answered.

"That sounds like our hearts. If they're hard, we don't get what we need to grow as believers. And if we don't grow, we won't win as many to Jesus." Nicolai looked pleased with his comparison. "Luke told us something like that, too. He told about a seed that fell on rocky ground, and although it grew quickly, it soon withered and died because it could not get moisture. Luke said that was like people who hear about Jesus' death, burial, and resurrection and accept it with joy; but because they have no true root, when they're tempted, they give up following Jesus."

"You're quite a little preacher, my boy," Justin teased. "If you and your mother had your way, every one of us on this farm would be a follower of Jesus."

"That would be a fine thing." Nicolai beamed.

Justin kept on plowing back and forth in the narrow field.

Nicolai looked at him wistfully. He was such a good friend. Why wouldn't he believe in Jesus?

The day's plowing was at last finished. Nicolai hurriedly ate a lunch of leftovers and headed out the door to find Tracker. "Here, boy! Come on, Tracker," he called and then whistled. His faithful companion came running, seeming to sense that the hunt was about to begin. Justin and Alexander soon joined him and off they went through a wooded area by a picturesque stream that gurgled through the woods and into the tangled brambles that grew next to an open field. They hoped to rouse up a hare from its hiding place in the briars. Tracker ran ahead, then ran back and circled the trio, and finally scampered off again. They were picking their way through the thorny bushes, being careful not to smack each other with a flying branch of tiny spears, when Tracker put his nose to the ground and started running this way

"HE'S ON TO A HARE."

and that. "He's on to a hare," Justin told Nicolai. "See, he's following its scent." Tracker ran with his nose to the ground for several minutes giving long, deep barks as he went. They watched as the sleek cream-colored animal disappeared. Suddenly, the barking stopped.

"Let's go see what he's up to," Justin said. "I think our hare has outsmarted Tracker," he said, laughing as they came back to the stream. "Looks like she circled back around, and Tracker lost the hare's scent again."

"Let's try the field again," Alexander suggested. "The hares love it out there where they can eat our crops."

Nicolai hoped they could get a hare, but he honestly enjoyed just being outdoors in the fresh air and sunshine. Thus even when they had spent an hour with no more signs of a hare, he didn't feel discouraged. Tracker was restless and kept dashing from one direction to another with his nose sniffing as he went. Finally, he was on the run again after

"I CAN DO IT."

catching another fresh scent.

The hunters stood stock-still, waiting for the hare to circle back around as Tracker gave chase. Their patience was rewarded when the hare bounded into sight, taking great leaps in its attempt to outdistance the determined dog.

Alexander raised his bow to shoot, but Justin signaled him to put it down. "Let Nicolai try." He mouthed the words.

Nicolai fumbled with his bow as he shook with excitement. "I can do it," he told himself as he carefully aimed and let the arrow fly.

"I got him! I got him!" he shouted as he ran to get his prize. "Won't Mother be surprised?" In all the country, a prouder lad would have been difficult to find.

Alexander thought they should start back to the house then even though Nicolai was itching to keep going now that he had one trophy. Alexander reminded him that it was a long walk back to the house, and they still had to check on the shepherds and sheep. Nicolai reluctantly agreed.

Nicolai sat perched on a boulder high on the hillside above the farm buildings as Alexander spoke with the shepherds. He couldn't understand how they could talk about sheep so much. Sheep were such dumb animals. They would wander off and get lost if the shepherds didn't watch them every minute. He didn't think they were valuable for their wool and meat. Alexander could take care of that business. He wasn't interested.

As Nicolai sat staring into the distance, he could see the great Egnatia Highway, which looked like a tiny ribbon, winding its way through a patchwork of fields and woods. Then, to his right, as far as he could see, a light flashed and kept shining as it moved closer to him on that ribbon of highway. What could it be? "Alexander, come quickly!" Alexander sprinted to the spot, thinking his younger brother was in danger. "Look at the strange light moving on the highway!" Nicolai pointed it out excitedly.

Alexander studied it for some time and then grinned. "Looks like Philippi is getting more company. That's the reflection of the sun on the Roman soldiers' helmets," he announced.

"And I thought I'd discovered a great mystery," Nicolai said, pouting.

"One that wasn't too difficult to solve." Alexander laughed as he tousled Nicolai's hair.

"ONE THAT WASN'T TOO DIFFICULT TO SOLVE."

THE RAIN WAS COMING DOWN IN SHEETS. . . .

11

SICKNESS

The rain started suddenly, and Lydia's family wasn't prepared for the instant deluge. They were nearly back to Philippi when it came, but that didn't keep them from getting soaked. They pulled their cloaks closer to them and sprinted down the road with Alexander still leading Queen while Grandfather hunched down over her mane. The rain was coming down in sheets with the wind driving it into their faces so that no one noticed the great hole in the road until Queen's foot and leg went down in it and

Grandfather came tumbling off and onto the rock-paved highway. Rain quickly mixed with the blood that flowed from the cuts and scrapes inflicted by the rough pavement. The roadway was soon colored red. As Lydia and Nicolai came to his side, they could see that Grandfather's arm and leg had been badly cut.

"Nicolai, please hand me your cloak," Lydia requested, and she soon had the worst of the cuts on his arm bound. Then she used her own cloak to bind his leg.

Meanwhile, Alexander managed to get the frightened horse out of the hole. He was relieved to see that Queen was not lame. Grandfather protested when Alexander gave him his cloak to wear as additional protection from the wind. "Do you think I'm feeble?" he said.

"Oh, no, Grandfather," Alexander assured. "But you are special, and we want to help you. That was a pretty rough tumble you just took," he told him as he helped him back on the horse.

Even though they were close to home, the

"DO YOU THINK I'M FEEBLE?"

blinding rain slowed their progress, and when they finally came to the shelter of the house, they were thankful to have a roof over their heads and the rain out of their eyes. Four puddles formed where each one stood. A servant went to care for Queen while Lydia and the boys quickly changed into dry clothes; then Lydia went to care for Grandfather. She carefully cleaned his wounds and applied a mixture of honey and olive oil, which she then covered with a lint, a linen cloth that is scraped and softened.

They all ate a warm evening meal and made their way to bed. Lydia pulled the colorful coverlet around her shoulders. How wonderful it was to be warm and dry! She was soon lulled to sleep by the patter of rain on the roof.

When Lydia entered Grandfather's room the next morning to change the dressing on his wounds, she knew something was wrong. His breathing seemed very shallow and was often broken by harsh bouts of coughing. He briefly opened his eyes when

"QUICKLY, HURRY AND GET LUKE."

she entered the room, but that appeared to be too much effort for him; and he let them close again without speaking a word to Lydia. She rushed to his side and put her hand on his forehead. He was burning up!

"Grandfather has the fever," she informed Phebe. "Quickly, hurry and get Luke. I pray he'll know what to do. The fever has taken so many people, and Grandfather is not as young and strong as he once was. Oh, do hurry. Grandfather means so much to us. I don't want to lose him."

Fright showing on her face, Phebe hurried off in search of Luke. Luke examined the old man and then gently coaxed him to take some myrrh. He checked his wounds and found them to be healing nicely. There was no infection. When he reported that to Lydia, she was greatly relieved. "Thank you. I was so concerned that I hadn't cleaned the wounds properly," she said.

"I'm afraid there is a very serious problem, though," Luke continued. "He has the fever; and

SPIRO AND DIMITRI STOOD AT THE DOOR ASKING TO BE
PERMITTED TO SEE GRANDFATHER.

considering his age, that could be a very dangerous situation. Continue to give him medicine, but I'd advise you to be sure everything is in order with his will in case he doesn't come through this."

Lydia put her head down, and her chin began to quiver. "We'll do all we can for him," she promised.

When Luke left the room, she gathered her boys and the servants in the courtyard and explained Grandfather's condition, and they all prayed. No sooner had they finished when Nicolai said, "Let's ask all of the Christians to pray."

"That sounds like the only answer at this time," Lydia said. "Run and tell all of the church members." Off Nicolai went, satisfied that he was doing the best thing he could for his grandfather.

Grandfather stirred a little when he heard a commotion at the entry. It had only been an hour since Nicolai had left with his prayer request, and now Spiro and Dimitri stood at the door asking to be permitted to see Grandfather. Lydia had great reservations about permitting them in, but they

LYDIA CHOSE TO STICK CLOSE BY THE ROOM.

assured her that they had come as friends. It was true that at one time Grandfather had been a friend to them, but she had felt that it had been a one-sided friendship. When he could still hear well, Grandfather had enjoyed talking to everyone.

"You may go, but only for a short time. He is very ill."

"We understand that," they agreed.

Lydia chose to stick close by the room. At first, the voices coming from the room were low; but, of course, Grandfather could not hear them because of his hearing problem. It didn't take Spiro long to speak loudly and distinctly to get his point across. "You see, it would be to your benefit to will your business to us and make us executors. Since your only child is a woman and her boys are too young to run the business, you could entrust it to us, and we would see to the care of the family. Since we have a similar business, we would have no trouble running the business successfully. We've brought the papers with us. You know Lydia is having a hard time making a go of the business now, and we'd love to turn that around for them."

Grandfather shut his tired eyes and did not respond.

Lydia, who had heard everything, stepped in and quietly announced, "You must leave now. Grandfather needs all the rest he can get if he's going to get over this."

"Just give us another minute with him, Lydia. We'd like to say good-bye in case he doesn't make it."

Lydia reluctantly agreed. What harm could come of a good-bye?

She stepped out and heard, "The papers are in the chest. We'll give you time to think about it, and we'll come back. Remember, it's your responsibility to see to the care of your family. This is the only way to do it. As your friends, we'd be happy to take this responsibility for you. We know you'd do it for us, too, if we were in the same situation."

"EPAPHRODITES, IT'S SO GOOD TO HAVE YOU BACK."

12

EPAPHRODITES'S RETURN

Grandfather had shown little improvement over the past week; but Lydia knew she had to go back to the shop to care for the business, so she left him in the care of the faithful servants. She was busy adding figures when she heard an "Ahem" and looked up to see their old friend, Epaphrodites, standing right in front of her. He looked happy, but without his normal sparkle. As a matter of fact, he actually reminded her of Grandfather.

"Epaphrodites, it's so good to have you back. We

had heard that you've been sick. I'm glad you're well enough to come back to us. How is Paul? Did you get the money to him safely? How was your journey?"

"My journey was uneventful for which I'm grateful. I have a surprise for you, though." He pulled a scroll from his girdle and handed it to her. "Here, a letter from Paul himself. Luke has read it and plans to read it in the next service, but he thought you would be interested in reading it now."

Epaphrodites retreated to the back room to visit with old Lucius while Lydia sat down to read the letter. How wonderful it was to hear from Paul again! She began to devour every word. She had read and reread every word several times before Epaphrodites reappeared.

"Epaphrodites, you certainly have gone the extra mile for us in taking our messages and offering to Paul. I'm thankful that God in His grace spared your life and allowed you to return to us. The next time, you must take someone with you so that you won't be so overworked. Paul says you nearly died. What happened?" Lydia asked.

"I guess I was exhausted from the journey. The weather was not favorable in the beginning, and I tried to help encourage the Christians in the churches along the way. They have so many questions; and since I've spent so much time with Luke, I felt I could help them. However, the rest was a luxury for me; and as a result, I was exhausted when the caravan reached Rome."

"How terrible," Lydia cried.

"True, but it wasn't terrible," Epaphrodites continued. "It was a time for me to grow closer to Jesus and depend on Him so now I know and love Him even more. I'm grateful it happened and am thankful for all the prayers of the saints."

"Now you sound like Paul. It makes me feel ashamed for complaining and worrying about petty things like the business," Lydia commented. "Why, Paul is praising God because he's in prison; and, as a result, people in the palace have heard of Jesus, and others are becoming bolder in their witness.

"PEOPLE IN THE PALACE HAVE HEARD OF JESUS."

Then he says, 'For to me to live is Christ, and to die is gain.'

"This should inspire us to do as he says and to be united and to strive together for the gospel. We all need to be servants, just as Christ was, so that we can shine as lights in this world darkened by sin. Did you see what he said toward the end of the letter?" she asked without giving Epaphrodites a chance to answer. "We are to rejoice in the Lord and be content no matter what our circumstances. Well, our circumstances are certainly more tolerable than Paul's, and I know God can and will work through our congregation if we don't get discouraged."

LYDIA CONSIDERED HER OPTIONS AND THEIR RESULTS.

13

SPECIAL NEED

Lydia was rejoicing in the Lord, but her concern showed on her face as she wrinkled her brow and went back to rework the figures that she had just reworked three times.

"Mother, is it serious?" Alexander asked as his mother pushed the paper from her and sat chin in hand as she considered her options and their results.

"Yes, Alexander, I'm afraid it is. Business is dropping off more rapidly than ever; and if something doesn't turn around soon, we may lose everything—

our business, home, perhaps the farm. As it is, I must let some of the workers go. There is no work for them if we have no business, and there is certainly no money with which to pay them. That hurts the most. They depend on their work here to support their families. We must pray that they find work without difficulty, but it won't be easy since most of the businessmen have slaves and feel that's much cheaper labor for them."

"How do they do it, Mother?" asked Nicolai.

"Who? Do what?" asked Lydia.

"You know—Spiro and Dimitri—how do they get to all of the customers first, Mother?"

"And how do they get them to buy that second-rate material over our fine linen and wool?" added Alexander.

"That's a mystery that I haven't quite been able to solve yet. Spiro always seems to know when a prospective customer is coming to Philippi before he even gets here. That could be a key to saving our business if we could just discover what it was."

"LYDIA, I HAVE A QUESTION FOR YOU."

Their conversation was interrupted by the appearance of one of their steady customers. "Lydia, I have a question for you," he began.

"Yes?" Lydia prompted.

"You know I'm not one to beat around the bush, so I'll just come right out with it. I thought it only fair that I talk to you before I take my business elsewhere."

Lydia looked bewildered but nodded for him to go on while thinking the business would surely die if she lost his business, too.

"A friend of mine just told me that this sect to which you belong—called Christians, I believe—is conspiring to overthrow Rome. Now, you know that I'm Roman through and through and proud that Philippi is part of a Roman colony. I will not support any business that would contribute to a cause that plans to overthrow the Roman Empire. Perhaps because you were married to a Jew and your children are part Jewish, you feel this is the thing to do, but I must separate myself from it."

"Oh, thank you for coming to me first," Lydia said gratefully. She then began to tell him all she knew about Jesus and ended by saying, "So you see, the kingdom we seek is not of this earth, but of heaven. Jesus Himself admonished us to obey those in authority in the world, and believers are encouraged to be law-abiding citizens. You are welcome to come to our services and find out for yourself if what I tell you is true or not. For now, the services are in my home; but that may soon have to end, so I would suggest you come to the next service."

"I might do that, but I believe you're telling me the truth. Tell me, why would you stop the services from being held in your home if all you say is true?"

"I wouldn't stop them, but my business is no longer profitable; and I'm afraid I'm going to lose my home along with my business if things don't change soon. At least now I know why so many of my customers have been dealing with Spiro and

"THERE IS A HUGE CARAVAN
DUE IN PHILIPPI TOMORROW."

Dimitri. If I can stop this rumor, it's bound to help business; but a rumor once started is a very difficult thing to stop."

"I'll do what I can to spread the truth," assured the customer. "In the meantime, you might be interested to know that there is a huge caravan due in Philippi tomorrow. They are coming from Rome, and I've been told by a friend that there will be nobility among them. One of the things they're looking for is a fine purple fabric that they've heard is manufactured in this area."

Lydia's face brightened as he talked.

"I'd recommend that you be out there to meet that caravan when it arrives. I know that your competitor, Spiro, always waits at the gates when a caravan arrives and soon has any buyers eating out of his hand. He's a pretty shrewd businessman, but your product is a much finer quality; and I'm sure you'll have a big sale if Spiro doesn't get to them first. I know that I'm happy that I can still do business with you. Have a good day."

And saying that, he was gone.

Lydia, Alexander, and Nicolai just sat and stared out the door for several minutes after he walked through it.

Right when it had seemed that everything was about to fall apart, God had provided a solution to their problem. Now, they had to get busy and find a plan that would be sure to end Spiro and Dimitri's conspiracy. It would never do to wait at the gate where Spiro was sure to be—especially since nearly the whole city thought they were planning an overthrow of the Romans. What could they do?

14

SECRET WEAPON

"Nicolai, it's time. Wake up," whispered Alexander. Nicolai felt the urgency in his brother's voice and remembered the plan they had formulated the night before. He rubbed his tired eyes, pushed back his tapestry-adorned cover, and jumped to his feet. As his feet touched the cold, tile floor, he howled and jumped back into bed. Tracker rose slowly from his spot at the bottom of Nicolai's bed and opened his mouth in a wide yawn. The old dog ambled over to Nicolai's bedside, put his large paw on the bed

"NICOLAI, IT'S TIME. WAKE UP."

beside Nicolai's head, and cocked his head with a pleading, "Please get up and help" look.

"Okay, okay. I'm up. See, my feet are on the floor," he defended as his toes once again touched the cold floor. He quickly slid the sandals and robe on and concealed the secret weapon in the folds of his robe. From the courtyard came the smell of freshly baked wheat bread, and his nose took him directly to the scent. The cook had prepared enough provisions to last the day. If more were needed, they would be on their own after they'd reached the farm.

Now wide awake, it was exciting for Nicolai as they left the shelter of home and stepped out into the quiet darkness of early morning. An eerie silence enveloped them as they walked the abandoned streets past darkened homes and shops toward the great Egnatia Highway. What if Spiro and Dimitri suspected them? What if they followed them? Nicolai hastened his steps past every darkened street corner. They didn't talk, but he noticed that Alexander hurried past those shadowy hiding places, too. Reaching the highway, they followed it to the gate of Philippi and beyond. One-half mile out of the city, they left the main road for a trail that would lead them to the foothills of their farm.

Dawn was breaking darkness's black hold on their world as they reached the country house. Nicolai whispered a prayer for a day of sunshine. Pointing to an outcropping of rock beyond the terraces and high on the steep hillside, Alexander instructed Nicolai to station himself there as quickly as possible. Alexander would be in the big, open courtyard of the home. Nicolai felt much safer now that he was on his grandfather's land and the darkness had given way to a new day's light. He relaxed and enjoyed the gentle breeze that caused the olive leaves on their gnarled old branches to shimmer from silver to gray and quickly back to silver. He climbed the hill straight up to the terraces with their vineyards, orchards, and vegetable gardens. A steep set of old stone steps joined the layered terraces. Beyond the terraces, a little-used path wound its way up

THEY LEFT THE MAIN ROAD FOR A TRAIL.

through the barren countryside. Nicolai's feet were dusty and tired, so he decided to rest for just a few minutes by a little mountain stream. He didn't want to waste any time, though, lest their plans should fall into complete ruin. Into his mouth he plopped some juicy grapes that he had picked on the last terrace. What a delightfully sweet taste! He was contemplating going back for more when he was startled by a sudden crack. Instead of going back, he quietly rose to his feet and started walking resolutely up the winding path. He didn't want to look back over his shoulder, but he had the strangest feeling that he was being followed. *Shake it off—it's probably nothing,* he assured himself. *Maybe one of the sheep has wandered off from the flock—the shepherds need to be more watchful,* he thought.

The eerie feeling didn't go away. To prove to himself that there was nothing to fear, he whirled around suddenly. There was nothing. Or was that bush shaking more than it should be? His heart was beating faster; and although the path was steeper

HE HAD THE STRANGEST FEELING THAT
HE WAS BEING FOLLOWED.

now, he hastened his steps. What was he going to do? If someone or something attacked up here, surely there would be no one to help. *Don't be silly*, he told himself, *you're just borrowing trouble*. He walked swiftly through the stand of trees. Open areas seemed more secure.

"Ba–a–a!" A goat! What a relief!

"You pest! Have you been stalking me?" Nicolai laughed with relief and headed for the rock the nimble goat had perched itself upon.

"Why would you be worried about being stalked?" Nicolai spun around to face the cynical eyes of Dimitri. "You trying to hide something?"

"I'm afraid you're trespassing on my grandfather's property," Nicolai almost shouted, "and I'm asking you to leave right now."

"I'll be glad to oblige you as soon as you show me what you're hiding in the folds of your robe."

Nicolai took a step back, held on to his side, and protested, "It's really not something I can share with you."

Snarling, Dimitri pulled a knife from a sheath at his side and instantly had it at Nicolai's throat. "This knife tells me you'll see things my way. I want to see it now," he demanded.

Looking over his shoulder, Nicolai knew he couldn't run. He had backed to the edge of a high rock. The knife at his throat made him gulp. His mind was racing. The thought of his mother and grandfather losing their home and business was horrible—and what about the church? How could he let this happen to the church? Where would they meet now? It would be his fault if the plan failed, but he had no option except to show Dimitri. "Help me please, Lord," he quietly prayed as he pulled the object from the folds of his garment.

"A mirror! I followed you all the way up here for a mirror?" scoffed Dimitri. "Off with a gift for some pretty little shepherd girl, I presume? It's no wonder your grandfather's business is falling apart. He should have never allowed your mother to convince him to give the slaves their freedom.

"A MIRROR!"

There must be a separation of the classes. Now, here is her son chasing a lowly shepherd girl who should be his slave. I suppose you'll want to choose your own wife instead of allowing your mother and grandfather to make those arrangements properly. There is your grandfather lying sick in bed, and you're out here making a mockery of his good family name. Rest assured, your grandfather will hear of this," Dimitri scolded as he returned his knife to the sheath and turned to go back to the Egnatia Highway.

Nicolai stood on the rock dumbfounded. The goat jumped to another ridge as if wanting out of the whole mess. Finally, Nicolai regained his senses and hurried to the outcropping of rocks that Alexander had directed him to just a short time earlier. He needed to hurry. They could be coming any time now, and he didn't want to let his family and the church down. A half hour later, he had dropped to the rock outcropping and was ready to keep his vigil of watching, whether they appeared in the next

NICOLAI WAS READY TO KEEP HIS VIGIL OF WATCHING.

instant or in another week. He hoped Dimitri hadn't spotted Alexander, and he hoped it didn't occur to him that the mirror was part of a plan.

THE REFLECTION OF THE SUN'S LIGHT ON THE MIRROR.

15

ROYAL GARMENTS

The sun beat down on Nicolai, and great beads of perspiration formed on his forehead and ran down the sides of his face. "I'm glad I'm not plowing today," he said to himself. Bored, he began to sing some of the songs he had been taught in school and then went on to the ones he'd been learning in church. All the while, he kept a constant vigil. He knew this could be the turning point for the business. The bleating of a goat drew his attention away for just a second; but when he turned back, he could see the glint of the Roman soldiers' helmets—they were on their way to Philippi!

Immediately, Nicolai pulled out his mirror and, using the reflection of the sun's light on the mirror, signaled his brother, who had also been keeping vigil far below in the courtyard of the country house. Alexander signaled back; and when Nicolai saw the tiny light flashing far below him, he knew that the plan was finally going into action.

Alexander spoke quickly to a servant, who left immediately on Queen, going east toward Philippi. Alexander left on foot going west. An hour later, he sighted the caravan that was steadily making its way towards Philippi. A prayer on his lips, Alexander walked with more determination. So much depended on this sale. Alexander quickly made friends with a Jewish businessman in the caravan and was able to learn the name of the lady who had come to buy the purple cloth for the nobility of Rome. He invited his new friend to his home for the evening meal and hurried off to find Junia.

ALEXANDER QUICKLY MADE FRIENDS....

"Do you know Junia from Rome?" he questioned some young man.

"Up behind the soldiers. They watch her closely, for she is a friend of a prominent senator's wife." Hesitating only a second, Alexander marched to the group behind the soldiers. He knew he had to talk to Junia.

"Excuse me. Would you happen to be Junia?" he questioned the lady who fit the description given to him by his Jewish friend.

"And if I am?" she returned.

"I have purple fabric I would like to show you, with your permission," Alexander announced.

"I am Junia." She smiled at him, and that relieved some of the tension that Alexander had felt building. Perhaps this wouldn't be so bad after all.

"Please notice the number of threads as compared to that of our competitors." He pulled out two pieces of cloth—one of their own and one that had been purchased from the shop of Spiro and Dimitri.

"I AM JUNIA."

"Yes, I see, and the color is beautiful!"

"My mother manages the shop. She has freed the slaves and feels their work is of a higher quality because they are not forced to do the job but work because they choose to work."

"Ah, that sounds like wise management to me," Junia praised. "And I know Someone who can set you and your mother free from the power of sin."

Alexander stared at her in amazement. "You're talking about the Lord Jesus, aren't you?"

"Yes, I am," Junia replied. "You've heard of Him?"

"Most definitely," Alexander responded. "Our whole family has accepted Him as Savior. He is the Master of our lives and has changed our lives completely. Junia, does this mean that you, too, are a Christian?"

"I am, and I'm thrilled that I shall be dealing with Christians on this trip. I'm very eager to meet your mother now."

They talked about Lydia and Philippi until they neared the gate of the city. Alexander could see

"THESE PEOPLE BELONG TO THE SECT
CALLED CHRISTIANS."

Spiro making his way towards Junia. A look of shock came over him when he saw Alexander, but he squared his shoulders and came on anyway. This was a complication that Spiro had not anticipated; but he knew he was more experienced at this than Alexander, so he didn't overly concern himself.

"I hear you are in Philippi to buy fabric?"

"Yes, I am," Junia replied.

"My friend has the best in the city. Allow me to take you to his shop," Spiro continued.

So that was their line, thought Alexander.

"I'll be glad to look at it after I go to Lydia's shop. I'm sure she can direct me there."

Spiro looked at Alexander, looked away, and then started whispering to Junia. "I'm sure you'd want to know that these people belong to the sect called Christians. I've heard from reliable sources that they have plans to overthrow the Roman government. Being a loyal Roman citizen, I'm sure you'll want nothing to do with them. Many of their long-standing customers have left them for that very reason and are now buying from my friend."

""What a shame," sympathized Junia. "I've always felt Christians were an asset to the empire. I am one myself."

Spiro stopped dead in his tracks, shut his eyes, and grimaced.

It took all of the willpower Alexander could muster to hold back the chuckle. Junia didn't try to hold hers back.

Lydia had prepared the shop well, and it was impressive to Junia to see all of the workers happily doing the jobs assigned them. Lucius's toothless smile gave her a big welcome. Junia and Lydia were instant friends. The sale that Lydia made that day was enough to keep them in business for a year, and she was confident that having the approval of Roman nobility would bring back business that had been lost because of the rumors of disloyalty.

Junia made the promised trip to Spiro and Dimitri's shop and wisely advised them to improve the quality of their cloth or find another business.

JUNIA AND LYDIA WERE INSTANT FRIENDS.

Lydia invited Junia and all those with her to her home while they were in Philippi. At the evening meal, she was finally able to ask her what she'd been longing to know. Alexander was glad his new Jewish friend was there to hear the conversation. Grandfather surprised everyone by joining them for the first time since the accident.

Lydia didn't wait long to ask, "How did you come to accept Christ as Savior when you live in Rome, where Nero persecutes the Christians?"

"That is just it. Nero tortures them, but they still cling tenaciously to their faith in Christ, especially the apostle Paul. Many soldiers had contact with him, and one who was chained to Paul taught me all that he learned from Paul. I know what these people say is true, or they wouldn't suffer as they do for Christ. How could I do anything but accept Jesus as Savior?"

"So you know of Paul?" Lydia asked. "He is a friend of ours. He told my household about Christ and baptized us. Do you have any word of him?"

Junia dropped her eyes for a few seconds, drew a deep breath, and looked compassionately at Lydia. "I'm sorry to tell you this. They have beheaded him."

Tears filled Lydia's eyes. Were they tears of sadness or tears of joy? She did not know, but she did know that Paul's own words kept playing over and over in her head. "For me to live is Christ; to die is gain."

Her friend Paul had gained his place in heaven. God was to be glorified.

"FOR ME TO LIVE IS CHRIST; TO DIE IS GAIN."

16

VISIT OF THE ROMAN SOLDIER

Out of the corner of her eye, Lydia noticed the tall Roman soldier walk into the shop as she was discussing Grandfather's steady recovery with a concerned church member. There was always something unnerving about the presence of a Roman soldier in her shop, even though there were always soldiers coming and going in Philippi. She excused herself from her friend and approached the soldier. "May I help you?"

"ARE YOU LYDIA OF THYATIRA?"

"Are you Lydia of Thyatira?" he questioned.

"Yes, I am, sir," she replied, taken aback by the fact that he was specifically looking for her.

"Then I have news for you from Caesarea."

At the mention of the city in which her husband had lost his life, Lydia turned as white as a sheet; and she felt she must sit down. "Please come back to the workroom," she invited. The Roman seemed grateful when she offered him a chair by an old wooden table. "The news from Caesarea?" Lydia wanted to know, but was afraid to learn.

"You see," the soldier began, "I have been a Roman soldier for many years now. My first assignment as a centurion was in Jerusalem. I thought that was the worst fate that could befall me, but it was the turning point in my life. There, I was assigned to the crucifixion of the Jewish teacher, Jesus."

Lydia's eyes grew wide. Could she trust this soldier? He seemed quite trustworthy—but the man who crucified Jesus?

"The circumstances were so unusual. One

week, He had a huge following; and the next—the same crowd demanded His death. The accusation that they put over His head when they crucified Him was: THIS IS JESUS, THE KING OF THE JEWS; and when the chief priest tried to get Pilate to change the sign to 'He said, "I am King of the Jews," ' Pilate answered, 'What I have written, I have written.'

"The crowd continued to mock Him, but He seemed so innocent to me. He even asked God to forgive us for crucifying Him. He said we didn't understand what we were doing. And then, in the middle of the day—the sixth hour—an unnatural darkness surrounded us until the ninth hour. I felt as if the very presence of God had been taken from the face of the earth.

"At the last, Jesus cried out, 'Father, into Thy hands I commend My spirit,' and He was gone. I knew at that instant who the man was and fell on my knees at that cross and cried out, 'Truly this man was the Son of God.'

"HE GAVE ME A MESSAGE FOR YOU."

"I was marveling at all that had happened when a Hermes of Thyatira and more recently of Philippi approached me."

At the mention of her husband's name, Lydia raised her head and gasped, "You met my husband?"

"Yes, and I talked to him just before he died. He gave me a message for you. In all of my years as a soldier, this has been my first opportunity to come to Philippi, so the message has been delayed far too long.

"As you probably know, he was in Jerusalem to sell your purple fabric and to buy grain from Israel and precious jewels brought to Jerusalem by other traders. He was caught in the crowd that moved along the Via Dolorosa to Calvary and witnessed the crucifixion. There, he saw me as I fell to my knees at the cross. He felt Jesus was innocent of any crime, but wasn't sure what to make of His claims that He was the Messiah. He was still pondering all of these things when he had to hurry off to celebrate the Feast of Unleavened Bread with acquaintances of his.

"The next time I saw him was outside the walls of Caesarea. As his caravan had neared Caesarea, he had fallen behind the rest while discussing business with a fellow traveler. It seems this traveler was actually a bandit who left your husband for dead. As I traveled towards Caesarea a few hours later, I saw him lying there and didn't even recognize him until I went to help.

"And what do you think he wanted to know? He asked if I had learned any more of the man called Jesus. Did I ever have exciting news for him! The chief priests had requested that guards be stationed at Jesus' tomb. Can you imagine that? Guards for a dead man?"

Lydia shook her head in wonder as she listened spellbound.

The Roman soldier continued, "They said there were reports that Jesus said He would rise from the dead after three days. I sent my most reliable men to the grave because I was curious to know what would happen. After three days, the body was gone! The men said they fell asleep, but I knew them better than that—they had been paid off—of that I am sure. Then, there were reports that Jesus had been seen by many in and around Jerusalem.

"Just before Hermes died, he said, 'Yes, He is the Son of God. Please. . .tell. . .Lydia.' And then, with a peaceful smile, he died."

He looked to see tears glistening in Lydia's eyes. "Thank you so much. It is an answer to prayer. You see, a little over ten years ago, an apostle of Jesus Christ, Paul, came to Philippi; and I was converted to Christianity. The Christians meet in my home to worship. My only sadness had been that my husband died before we heard the wonderful news of Jesus, but you have brought an answer to prayer that seemed impossible. Won't you please come to our services this week? Our congregation would surely love to hear about your conversion and that of my husband."

"GOD'S WAYS ARE TRULY WONDERFUL."

"There's a Christian church in Philippi?" questioned the Roman soldier. "This sounds like the perfect place for me to be stationed. If the congregation is willing, I'll join the church at the next service. God has been so good to me."

"Yes, God's ways are truly wonderful," Lydia agreed.